LET US PRAY

MAYOKUN OREOFE

LET US PRAY
Copyright © 2019 by Mayokun Oreofe

Published in Nigeria by
Mayokun Oreofe Ministry
www.mayokunoreofeministry.org
info@mayokunoreofeministry.org

+234 (0) 708 045 9144,
+234 (0) 815 679 1203
Facebook & Instagram:
@mayokunoreofeministry

All Rights Reserved.
Except for brief excerpts for review purposes,
no part of this book may be reproduced or used in any
form without written permission from the publisher.

Unless otherwise noted,
all Scripture quotations have been taken from different
versions of the Holy Bible; KJV, NKJV, NIV, NLT, ESV,
TPT, AMP, NASB, NET

ISBN: 978-978-56745-7-6

The Author is represented by
Mayokun Oreofe Ministry.

Printed in The Federal Republic of Nigeria
First Print 2019

CONTENT

Acknowledgement	v
Dedication	vii
Be Warned	viii
Introduction	ix
Let Us Pray	xviii

Chapter 1: I Give Thanks	1
Chapter 2: Have Mercy On Me Oh Lord	7
Chapter 3: Guide Me, Lead Me Every Day	13
Chapter 4: Deliver Me From Rebellion	19
Chapter 5: Open Your Hands Lord And Satisfy My Desires	24
Chapter 6: Give Me Your Wisdom Lord	31
Chapter 7: I Will Be Taught Of The Lord	39
Chapter 8: Restore My Fortunes And Decorate My Life	46
Chapter 9: My Ears Will Hear You Lord	53
Chapter 10: I Shall Lack Nothing	61
Chapter 11: Deliver Me, O Lord!	72
Chapter 12: My Help Comes From The Lord	81
Chapter 13: Hear My Prayers Lord.	92

CONTENT

Chapter 14: Lord, Remember Me This Day — 102

Chapter 15: Let There Be Light! — 111

Chapter 16: Grant Me Success Oh Lord! — 119

Chapter 17: Give Me Your Understanding Lord — 126

Chapter 18: Joy Unlimited! — 133

Chapter 19: A New Heart, A New Spirit! — 140

Chapter 20: Peace! — 147

Chapter 21: No Anxiety — 156

Chapter 22: Turn The Wicked Back To You Lord — 163

Chapter 23: Arise To My Defense O God! — 170

Chapter 24: Commitment To Serve — 179

Chapter 25: Grace For Humility — 188

ACKNOWLEDGEMENT

I thank God Almighty the One Who wrote in the 'SCRIPT' of my life that (prayer) will be my path, to the intent that He will inspire me to pen down His will for His people to pray.

I also express my heartfelt gratitude to my beloved husband, Pastor Olakunle Oreofe and my darling covenant children - Oluwajomiloju and Oluwadamiloju Oreofe; my greatest supporters and encouragers on this side of eternity. You have been my cheer leaders on the path of destiny. So much sacrifices you've had to make just to ensure I do God's bidding. I love and appreciate you all. Bonded we shall forever remain in Christ Jesus.

To these dynamic people whom the Lord brought on board my destiny vehicle for this divine instruction, I am truly grateful; Oluwaseun AyanfeOluwa, Florence Adewusi, and Doyin Akinwunmiju. You are my 'Bezaleels'. Jehovah will reward your tireless input and labour on this project.

Last but not the least to Sola Adesakin, a God given help and encourager on this mission to spew out my content in print. Sola your voice echoed in me till I rose to the task; and now that am here. I cannot but bless God for such inspiration that you are. Thank you for everything. Your destiny will not drag.

Truly grateful!

DEDICATION

I dedicate this book to my grandfather, **Rev. (Dr.) A.T. Ola Olude**, a renowned Spirit-filled Methodist minister in his days; on whom the grace for this inspiration for a prayer book first rested.

And now I find myself stepping into the same grace as his; just like Apostle Timothy did step into the grace of his grandmother, Lois.

BE WARNED

You are holding in your hands a companion that will enhance your prayer life. This book will make you pray as you read.

This is a practical prayer book, not a theoretical teaching about prayer. This book prays the Word of God and not rhetorical words of men.

LET US PRAY!

INTRODUCTION

Beloved of God, I am not writing this book as one who has attained in the place of prayer; rather I am one of those that God's grace has found hence through whom His power finds expression in my weakness.

> 2 Corinthians 12:9 (TPT) says
> "My grace is always more than enough for you, and my power finds its full expression through your weakness."

This book and every other you will come across authored by me especially on the subject of prayer, are therefore birthed by GRACE and not expertise.

LET US PRAY

It is nothing but the truth that all believers are expected to communicate with our Maker (God of heaven and earth); and PRAYER is what that manner of communication is called. Generally communication can be achieved via several means for as long as parties involved are being reached; hence it can be relatively said that communication is not particularly a herculean task. This statement however isn't true when it comes to communicating with God. Really, it is expected to be the easiest and best communication, but because of the obvious powerful outcome of this exercise with God, satan has made it a burdensome feat just so many wouldn't engage in it, and thereby they are denied the power thereof.

    Prayer is said to be the master key. It is that access we have to God's unlimited resource of all kind. Prayer (which is supposed to be our leeway of accessing God and His bounties), has become for many a very frustrating venture for many reasons I can't delve into here. However, I need to mention this one reason why prayer has become burdensome to many people; and that is lack of answers to prayers. If something appears as a task and then you make effort to engage in the task, and yet the expected result is not achieved, then it can be frustrating and discouraging to re-embrace.

While there are several reasons behind unanswered prayer, thereby making it burdensome to so many people, one of the aims of this book is to help you address, through its presentation of the subject of prayer, ease in praying and getting tangible answers in the place of prayer thereby putting an end to frustration.

Jesus one day made his disciples realize that prayer is not meant to be a one-off or a rarely done practice. He said prayer must be ongoing - Luke 18:1 (NKJV),

> "Then He spoke a parable to them that men always ought to pray and not lose heart."

When it comes to the issue of prayer, you cannot afford to get tired of it; you are expected to keep its fire burning.

The communication tag line of God is 'keep on praying'. Ain't no stopping, keep it going. Talking to a man shouldn't be more fascinating than talking to God, the Creator of man. He knows all things that men claim to know and yet knows much more, deeper and wider than men. There is no knowledge of man that can outwit Him. If He knows much more than man, why should talking to man be more frequent than talking to the One Who has all answers at His disposal?

Prayer is continual. The New Living Translation (NLT) of the Bible says in 1 Thessalonians 5:17:

"Never stop praying."

The Passion Translation says:
"Make your life a prayer."

Oh wow! What an expression. Prayer is that much serious; so let your life be prayer. If one's life must be about prayer, it is very important then for there to be tangible and encouraging results from it. This implies that one must get right whatever makes prayers to be answered. The emphasis of this book is to ensure our prayer effort (prayer life) is not fruitless, thereby putting an end to frustration.

LET US PRAY

Matthew 12:33 (NKJV) says:
> "Either make the tree good and its fruit good, or else make the tree bad and its fruit bad; for a tree is known by its fruit."

This book is set to make your prayer life a good one, that is interesting, apt and encouraging.

Wondering how this will happen? Knowing the ingredient that makes a soup taste in a preferred way, and employing it while cooking, guarantees your soup tasting just as it is desired. This is where having a recipe comes in. For the purpose of our focus in this book, a key ingredient to answered prayers is praying the will of the One Who has the sole capacity of answering. Pressing the right button in the place of prayer is praying the very will of God. You can be sure that asking according to His Will in the place of prayer guarantees you that He will answer in line as you have prayed.

I John 5:14-15 (NKJV):
> "Now this is the confidence that we have in Him, that if we ask anything according to His will, He hears us. And if

LET US PRAY

we know that He hears us, whatever we ask, we know that we have the petitions that we have asked of Him."

Awesome! Very relatable isn't it? You have a mindset to give your son a bicycle, double carriage, which of course is more expensive than a single carrier. You get home and he comes to you to say what he wants for his birthday is a double carrier bicycle. There won't be any argument, you simply hear him, smile, nod in affirmation and thereafter he gets his bicycle at the right time. Simple as A, B, C! Imagine if it were another dimension of request. You have a mind to give him the double carrier bicycle and he comes to you crying that he wants your type of car. He may ask with tears, that won't yield to him his desire. Reason is that you know what is best for him and you already have a mind to get him just that. Now asking for what is outside of your will only guarantee him a continuous crying and frustration cry. This is how most of us are in the place of prayer.

LET US PRAY

1 John 5:14-15 (TPT):
> "Since we have this confidence, we can also have great boldness before him, for if we ask anything agreeable to his will, he will hear us. And if we know that he hears us in whatever we ask, we also know that we have obtained the requests we ask of him."

Once your prayer is in line with the word and will of God, it becomes like an ATM card to a funded account. Once the card holder punches in the correct Pin code, and a certain withdrawal amount within the account balance as well as withdrawal limit for the day, all things being equal with the system, there will be no issue with having his desire of withdrawing money met.

This explains why Jesus our perfect role model taught us to pray, saying;

> "In this manner, therefore, pray: Our Father in heaven, Hallowed be Your name. Your kingdom come. Your will be done On earth as it is in heaven."
> Matthew 6:9-10 (NKJV)

LET US PRAY

This world of ours is not our own idea. Creation as a whole is God's idea and since it is His idea, His idea is what He is out to see fill and fulfilled in the earth. He won't go contrary to Himself, hence it is humorously said that "God does not pay for the meal He didn't order."

In this book therefore, we will be praying the will of God. What is the will of God? His will is that which He has purposed, hence it is that which He has on His mind.

God has something on His mind? Yes, He does. That which is on His mind is His will.

> "Now He who searches the hearts knows what the mind of the Spirit is, because He makes intercession for the saints according to the will of God."
> Romans 8:27 (NKJV)

Holy Spirit our Helper, in helping our prayer life, prays the will of God. He being the Spirit of God is able to best access the will of God hence He prays it. This is also why praying in the Spirit is a gracious door to a fruitful prayer life. You can't go wrong in praying God's will when you pray in the

LET US PRAY

Spirit. The Holy Spirit says nothing else apart from what God has willed.

Another perk of this book's focus on prayer is, it is not a theoretical or prayer teaching book, rather it is a practical, 'read and pray' or 'pray as you read' book. This simply means as you read line by line through the pages of this book, you are actually praying, only that you are not closing your eyes. For the most part of this book, you will actually be praying the will of God as you read through. Glad to let you know this is a PRAYER BOOK.

Do you feel inadequate in yourself, not knowing how to bring it all together in the place of prayer, or are you just in the mode to pray and you need to pray aright? Whichever is your disposition, once it has to do with praying and you truly want to pray, then this is a companion of all times.

I wish you unprecedented results even as you engage the companionship of this book in your prayer exploits.

LET US PRAY!

...praying the Word;
the prayers that God answers.

I Give Thanks

Jehovah God, I am here to give to You what You most rightly deserve. Father, You are deserving of praise, of worship and thanksgiving.

According to Psalms 119:12a,
> "You deserve praise, O LORD! Who is the wise person that will hold back Your praises? Only fools are found on such tracks. I choose wisdom, therefore Father, I offer praise to Your Holy name. King of kings and Lord of lords. The One Who was, the One Who is and the One still to come. Everlasting Father, the Ancient of days; I lift up my voice to bless You Lord."

LET US PRAY

Psalm 103:1-3 says,

"Bless (affectionately, gratefully praise) the Lord, O my soul; and all that is [deepest] within me, bless His holy name! Bless (affectionately, gratefully praise) the Lord, o my soul, and forget not [one of] all His benefits."

Father, for all You have done, at this moment I shout hallelujah; I praise You Lord. You are the Doer of all that resounds in my life. From morning to evening, You are the God at work. You never sleep nor slumber on me. You are ever alert to watch over me and to deliver me. Daily I am a beneficiary of Your grace. You forgive my sins, You redeem me from the pit and from corruption. You dignify and beautify me.

Lord, You give me strength and cause me to live as an overcomer; You fight my battles o Lord; I cannot keep silent, hence Lord, I shout yet again, Hallelujah! What shall I render to You o Lord my Father. You have done so much that I cannot seem to tell it all.

LET US PRAY
_____

Yet, Psalms 56:12 says,

> "I will fulfill my vows to you, O God, and will offer a sacrifice of thanks for your help."

To this end Lord, my heart is set and intent on paying my vows of that which You deserve.

I give You thanks for every benefit I have received of You. God of heaven and earth, to You be all the glory and the honour. There is no other God in Your class. For the gift of life I can never thank You enough. For shelter, my God You are awesome [You are the Lord Who has not allowed me to become homeless]. You cover my nakedness and watch my back, Father I say thank You. You put food on my table, allowing me to be satisfied with Your nourishment, Lord I say thank You.

Psalm 105:1-2 says,

> "O give thanks unto the Lord, call upon His name, make known His doings among the peoples! Sing to Him, sing praises to Him; meditate on and talk of all His marvelous deeds and devoutly praise them."

LET US PRAY

Your name is Yahweh, the I AM THAT I AM... You take delight in fixing the puzzles of my life. Your deeds are past listing for they outnumber the retention of my brain. How so kind are You my Father and my God. You dethrone and enthrone, yet never make a mistake. Your decisions in my life are appropriate, hence ultimately giving You the glory.

Father, saying THANK YOU is an understated expression of my heart of gratitude. I honour and adore You today. Take the glory my ever faithful and true God, in the name of Jesus Christ. Amen!

NOTES

Lord, I am here to say thank you. For the gift of life, for your faithfulness that is ever sure. You the giver of life, the God that knows the end from the beginning, the God that never fails. You deserve ALL the Glory and power. Your name really should be praised 24/7. My wonderful and glorious redeemer.

TESTIMONY

Have Mercy On Me Oh God

"Yours, O LORD, is the greatness, The power and the glory, The victory and the majesty; For all that is in heaven and in earth is Yours; Yours is the kingdom, O LORD, And You are exalted as head over all."

I Chronicles 29:11

Of a truth O Lord, Yours is the glory, power and greatness. There is no other God besides or like You. Victory and Majesty belongs to You Father. You own all things in heaven and on earth. Nothing exists without Your knowledge. Father I

LET US PRAY

exalt You, Jehovah I exalt You. Be magnified. Take Your place as the true and real owner of the entire creation.

It is written in Psalms 95:2 :
> "Let us chime before His presence with thanksgiving; Let us shout joyfully to Him with psalms."

Therefore Lord, I access Your Holy presence with thanksgiving and gratitude flowing from my heart to You this day. I am thankful for the privilege of being yours and the access I have to Your Presence.

> "It is good to give thanks unto Jehovah, and to sing psalms unto thy name, O Most High".
> Psalm 92:1

I thank You exceedingly O Lord. For all You have done I am appreciative of. Too numerous to count are the good things You O Lord have done in my life. Thank You, Thank You, Thank You.

LET US PRAY

In II Peter 3:9, the Bible says,

> "The Lord is not slack concerning His promise, as some count slackness, but is longsuffering toward us, not willing that any should perish but that all should come to repentance."

Father, I come to true repentance before You this very day. I am sorry for all my shortcomings, my errors of omission and even those deliberate acts of wrong I have ever engaged in. Lord, let Your bowel of mercy and compassion flow to me this day. Overlook my errors I pray, because Your word says in Psalm 86:15,

> "...You, o Lord, are a God full of compassion, and gracious, longsuffering and abundant in mercy and truth."

Have mercy on me O God. I ask for Your kindness, Your favour, and Your gentleness upon me. Do not deal with me according to the multitude of my sins. You are a faithful God, You keep Your covenant of mercy to a thousand generations who love You.

LET US PRAY

Deuteronomy. 7:9 states
"And thou shalt know that Jehovah thy God He is God the faithful· God who keepeth covenant and mercy to a thousand generations with them that love Him and keep His commandments".

Lord, prove Your faithfulness in my life on all fronts and let Your name be glorified forever in the mighty and precious name of Jesus Christ. Amen.

NOTES

TESTIMONY

Guide Me, Lead Me Every Day

Eternal God my Father, I honour and adore You. I ponder and wonder like the people of old as stated in Isaiah 63:11,

> "His people remembered the ancient times. Where is the one who brought them up out of the sea, along with the shepherd of his flock? Where is the one who placed his Holy Spirit among them? I am thirsty for the encounter of old."

Lord, please place Your Holy Spirit among me. I crave for Your direction and guidance even as You did by Your Spirit to the children of Israel on their wilderness journey.

LET US PRAY

The Bible recalls in Nehemiah 9:19-20,

> "You, in Your great mercy and compassion, Did not abandon them in the wilderness; The pillar of the cloud did not leave them by day, To lead them in the way, Nor the pillar of fire by night, to light for them the way they should go. You [also] gave Your good Spirit to instruct them, You did not withhold Your manna from their mouth, And You gave them water for their thirst."

My Father, please do not abandon me on the journey of life. In Your great mercy and compassion, do not leave me nor forsake me. I ask intently, that You lead me in the way to go. Instruct me by Your good and Holy Spirit. You said in your word in Psalms 32:8 ...

> "I will guide you along the best pathway for your life. I will advise you and watch over you."

Jehovah, I submit myself as a willing horse to be guided by You along the best path way for my life.

LET US PRAY

You alone know what is best for me. Father, I crave for Your advise and counsel. Do not hold back from me in the name of Jesus Christ.

It is written in John 16:13
> "...when he, the Spirit of truth, comes, he will guide you into all truth. For he will not speak on his own authority, but will speak whatever he hears, and will tell you what is to come."

Lord, do not hold back Your Spirit from me, let Your Spirit come; and please guide me into all truth thereby. I refuse to be led by lying spirits. By Your Spirit open me up to what is to come that I may not be caught in the web of error. I pray for revelation knowledge by Your Spirit. My Father please do not hide from me.

The Psalmist says in Psalms 119:133,
> "Guide my steps by your word, so I will not be overcome by evil."

So say I now, O Lord God of all flesh. Let Your word guide my steps, that no evil may overwhelm me.

LET US PRAY

Be my guide continually, non-stop. Be my guide in all circumstances of life, guide me when I am dry, guide me till I am soaked and set in You.

Jehovah, guide me at all cost even as Your word says in Isaiah 58:11,

> "The Lord will guide you continually, giving you water when you are dry and restoring your strength. You will be like a well-watered garden, like an ever-flowing spring."

Father God, please restore my strength. Let me be like the well watered garden whose leaves remain green all year round. I trust Your Majesty to lead and guide me in the mighty name of Jesus Christ. Amen.

NOTES

TESTIMONY

Deliver Me From My Rebellion.

Almighty and everlasting Father, humbly do I come before Your throne, take out of me every seed of rebellion. Your word says in the book of 1 Samuel 15:23,

> "Rebellion is as sinful as witchcraft, and stubbornness as bad as worshiping idols..."

I will not fall into such error in the name of Jesus Christ.
Lord, all those who rebel against You grieve the Holy Spirit as the Bible records in Isaiah 63:10

LET US PRAY

"...they rebelled and grieved His Holy Spirit; Therefore He changed into their enemy, And He fought against them."

I vehemently refuse rebellion in my life. There is no foothold for rebellion in me. As the Lord lives, no action of mine will cause God to change position, becoming my enemy. It will not happen and will never be. Jehovah will not turn His back against me in the name of Jesus Christ.

Acts 7:51 says,
"You stiff-necked and stubborn people, uncircumcised in heart and ears, you are always actively resisting the Holy Spirit. You are doing just as your fathers did."

O Lord God, I depart from the path of the rebellious fathers of old. Help me and I will not rebel against my You nor Your precepts. What You want is what I will pursue.

Scriptures says in Proverbs 17:11:
"Evil people are eager for rebellion, but they will be severely punished."

LET US PRAY

I cry Lord,
> "Rescue me from my rebellion. Do not let fools mock me." [Psalms 39:8].

In the mighty name of Jesus Christ, Father rescue me from the clutches of a rebellious spirit. I am Yours.

NOTES

TESTIMONY

Open Your Hands Lord And Satisfy My Desires

O Lord my God, Jesus my role model in John 11:41b-42a said:

> "...I thank you, Father, that you listen to me. I know that you always listen to me..."

I also dare say to You, 'I thank You for always listening to me when I call'. Jehovah, I trust You that even as I pray today You, O Lord, will listen and answer me.

LET US PRAY
───────

1 John 5:14 says:
"...this is the confidence that we have in Him, that if we ask anything according to His will, He hears us."

The Bible also says in Proverbs 10:28,
"The hope of the righteous [those of honorable character and integrity] is joy, But the expectation of the wicked [those who oppose God and ignore His wisdom] comes to nothing."

I thank You for my hope will lead to joy. What I desire from You, Jehovah You will magnanimously grant unto me this day. I will not ask for emptiness because according to Isaiah 45:19b You said

"I did not say to the seed of Jacob,
"Seek Me in vain.""

Psalm 21:2 says,
"For you have given him his heart's desire; you have withheld nothing he requested."

LET US PRAY

Jehovah, You will give me my heart desire, and nothing that I request will you hold back from me. My desires are coming to pass in the name of Jesus Christ. Father, please grant my heart beat. What I want in You, O Lord let them begin to manifest one after the other in the name of Jesus Christ. Your word says in John 15:7,

> "If you abide in Me, and My words abide in you, you will ask what you desire, and it shall be done for you."

Your word my God, have I kept and nurtured, let what I desire from You be done with precision.

> "What the wicked fears will come upon him, But the desire of the righteous [for the blessings of God] will be granted." [Proverbs 10:24].

Jehovah I pray, grant my desire. (Express your heart desires to God now).

I refuse and reject fear. As the Lord my God lives, I cast out every form and similitude of fear brewing in me. No evil shall manifest in my life.

LET US PRAY

Only my godly desires will be expressed in the name of Jesus Christ. Father, as one with the righteousness of Christ, I beseech You that my hope shall bring me nothing short of joy.

Proverbs 13:12 says,
> "Hope deferred makes the heart sick, But when the desire comes, it is a tree of life."

My heart will not fall sick. I refuse weariness and depression, I will not cast off restraint. I remain hopeful, being assured that as I pray, my God will sprout the tree of life in me. My desires will come to fruition.

> "You open Your hand And satisfy the desire of every living thing," says Psalms 145:16.

My Father, open Your hand towards me and satisfy my desires in the name of Jesus Christ. You granted Eleazar his desires even while he was yet speaking; and he testified in Genesis 24:45:

> "Before I had finished praying, Rebekah

LET US PRAY

came with her jar on her shoulder. She went down to the spring and drew water. "So I asked her, 'May I have a drink?'"

My Father, You also gave Solomon his very heart desire and much more. You said to him in 2 Chronicles 1:11-12:

> "...Because your greatest desire is to help your people, and you did not ask for wealth, riches, fame, or even the death of your enemies or a long life, but rather you asked for wisdom and knowledge to properly govern my people 12) I will certainly give you the wisdom and knowledge you requested. But I will also give you wealth, riches, and fame such as no other king has had before you or will ever have in the future!"

My Father and my Lord, I pray that You will graciously grant my heart desire and cause all my godly plans to succeed, even as Psalm 20:4 says,

> "May he grant your heart's desires and make all your plans succeed."

NOTES

TESTIMONY

Give Me Your Wisdom Lord

Dear God, I declare just as said in Daniel 2:20,

> "Blessed be the name of God forever and ever, For wisdom and might are His."

Wisdom and might are Yours. There's no argument about the source of true wisdom my Father and my God. Job found it and said in Job 12:13,

> "But true wisdom and power are found in God; counsel and understanding are his."

LET US PRAY

Though Wisdom is Yours and can be found only in You, yet You are magnanimous enough to graft man into the pool of Your wisdom.

James 1:5 says,
> "If any of you lacks wisdom, let him ask of God, who gives to all liberally and without reproach, and it will be given to him."

Lord, without any shamefacedness, I cry out to You for wisdom. Such Wisdom as can only be found in You. I thirst not for the wisdom of this world or age, but I ask for Your wisdom, such as You deemed fit to fill Bezaleel with. You said,

> "Look, I have specifically chosen Bezaleel son of Uri, grandson of Hur, of the tribe of Judah. I have filled him with the Spirit of God, giving him great wisdom, ability, and expertise in all kinds of crafts." [Exodus 31:2-3].

O Lord, let it please You now to fill me with wisdom.

LET US PRAY

Father, You chose to deprive the ostrich of wisdom, though in speed she is swifter than the horse, yet according to the account of Job 39:17,

> "...God has deprived her of wisdom. He has given her no understanding."

I pray, may my portion never be like that of the ostrich. David in Proverbs 4:5a & 7 admonished his son Solomon saying:

> "Get wisdom...getting wisdom is the wisest thing you can do! And whatever else you do, develop good judgment."

Lord, I choose to pursue wisdom. I beseech You Lord for wisdom. You gave Joshua wisdom. The Bible says in Deuteronomy 34:9a,

> "...Joshua son of Nun was full of the spirit of wisdom, for Moses had laid his hands on him..."

You did not hold back wisdom from Solomon the king, hence it is recorded in 1 Kings 4:29-30,

LET US PRAY

> "God gave Solomon very great wisdom and understanding, and knowledge as vast as the sands of the seashore. In fact, his wisdom exceeded that of all the wise men of the East and the wise men of Egypt."

Father! Grant unto me exceeding wisdom beyond that of my contemporaries. Your word says in Luke 21:15

> "for I will give you a mouth and wisdom which all your adversaries will not be able to contradict or resist."

O Lord, even beyond naysayers, detractors and adversaries, give me the wisdom they cannot mock in the name of Jesus Christ.

Daniel and the other Hebrew boys were preferred ten times more as the Bible says in Daniel 1:20,

> "...in all matters of wisdom and understanding about which the king examined them, he found them ten

times better than all the magicians and astrologers who were in all his realm."

O Lord, make me far better by reason of Your wisdom in me.

Psalm 119:98-100 says,
"Your commands make me wiser than my enemies, for they are my constant guide. "I am wiser than all my teachers, because I think about your rules." I am even wiser than my elders, for I have kept your commandments."

O God, I desire to be wise, give me wisdom. If Jesus, my Lord and Savior increased in wisdom, Father I ask for continual increase of Your wisdom in my life. I confess Luke 2:52,

"And Jesus increased in wisdom and stature, and in favor with God and men."
and so I also increase in wisdom in the name of Jesus Christ.

LET US PRAY
———————

Proverbs 2:6 says,
   "...the Lord grants wisdom! From his mouth come knowledge and understanding."

Jehovah grant me Your wisdom I pray in the name of Your wise Son Jesus Christ. Amen!

NOTES

TESTIMONY

I Will Be Taught Of The Lord

My heavenly Father, I revere You. You are God all by Yourself; One Who knows all things, and One to Whom nothing is hidden. Your wealth of knowledge is beyond comprehension. I worship and adore You.

I humble myself, for the scripture says in Psalm 25:9,

> "He leads the humble in doing right, teaching them his way."

With all humility of heart, I ask Lord that you lead me in doing right and teach me your ways by

LET US PRAY

every means deployable in You. It is written in Psalms 94:12,

> "Joyful are those you discipline, Lord, those you teach with your instructions."

Father I crave that You teach me Your instructions, that in my life I will not run a riotous living. Give me the privilege of such joy that is experienced by those You discipline.

Proverbs 3:11 & 12 enjoins,
> "My child, don't reject the Lord's discipline, and don't be upset when he corrects you. 12) For the Lord corrects those he loves, just as a father corrects a child in whom he delights."

Out of Your loving kindness my Father, correct and discipline me as a child You love. I submit to Your teachings, instructions and directions. Cause my ears to hear Your voice, instructing me where to go and what to do. Do not leave me to myself. Isaiah 30:21 says,

> "Your own ears will hear him. Right behind you a voice will say, "This is the way you should go," whether to the right or to the left."

LET US PRAY

Jehovah God, let me hear You everywhere I go.

Father God, let my case not be like that of the children of Israel at a point on their journey when the Bible says,

> "For a long time Israel was without the true God and without a priest to teach them and without the teachings." [2 Chronicles 15:3].

Let my life not be scarce of Your teaching. Teach me o Lord, for I delight in being taught of You.

Psalm 86:11 says,
> "Teach me Your way, O LORD; I will walk in Your truth; Unite my heart to fear Your name."

How will I ever know, if I am not taught O Dear Lord?

> "Teach me to do your will, for you are my God. May your gracious Spirit lead me forward on a firm footing." [Psalms 143:10].

LET US PRAY

I enrol in Your school for life. I remain teachable because Your grace is all I need to succumb to learning of You. I take Your yoke upon me to be taught as it is written in Matthew 11:29,

> "Take my yoke upon you. Let me teach you, because I am humble and gentle at heart, and you will find rest for your souls."

I long for rest; Father teach me and I will find rest in doing right.

> "Every day Jesus went to the Temple to teach…" [Luke 21:37].

Lord Jesus, I am Your temple; daily impart knowledge into me, give me clear instructions, inform me, enlighten me, discipline me, drill me, school me, and coach me.

> "You are good and do only good; teach me your decrees." [Psalms 119:68].

Teach me by Your scripture for,
> "All Scripture is inspired by God and is useful to teach us what is true and to

make us realize what is wrong in our lives. It corrects us when we are wrong and teaches us to do what is right." [2Timothy 3:16].

Teach me by Your Representative - the Holy Spirit, for it is written in John 14:26,

> "...when the Father sends the Advocate as my representative - that is, the Holy Spirit - he will teach you everything and will remind you of everything I have told you."

Father,
> "Lead me in Your truth and teach me, For You are the God of my salvation; On You I wait all the day." [Psalms 25:5].

I wait eagerly to be taught of You Father, teach me as You alone can; this is my prayer in the name of Jesus Christ.

NOTES

TESTIMONY

Restore My Fortunes And Decorate My Life

O dear God, the Ruler of all times. You are such an orderly God, so much that You have ordained the events and happenings of every season. Ecclesiastes 3:1 says:

> "To everything there is a season, A time for every purpose under heaven."

Daniel talking about You said,
> "...He changes the times and the seasons..." [Daniel 2:21a].

LET US PRAY

Lord, I have come for a change that only You can effect. For it is written in Ecclesiastes 3:4 that there is,

> "A time to cry and a time to laugh. A time to grieve and a time to dance."

Father, I ask for my laughter season to be activated. You are the Lord that activated for Sarah, a season of laughter; for she said in Genesis 21:6,

> "God has made me laugh. Everyone who hears about this will laugh with me."

Jehovah God in Whom there is no shadow of turning, God Who is no respecter of persons, I know that what You have done for one You are able to do for another; therefore my Lord, bring me and my household into a season of endless laughter and merriment in the name of Jesus Christ. Job said:

> "He will once again fill your mouth with laughter and your lips with shouts of joy." [Job 8:21].

LET US PRAY

He also said,
 "You will laugh at destruction and hunger, and you will not fear the wild animals," [Job 5:22].

I believe it and confess now that "I shall laugh for my mouth is being filled with laughter therefore I shout for Joy". Hallelujah!
 Jehovah, do with me as You have graciously done to Your seeds; for the scripture says in Psalms 126:1 & 2,

 "When the Lord restored the fortunes of Zion, we were like those who dream."
 "Then our mouth was filled with laughter, and our tongue with shouts of joy; then they said among the nations, "The Lord has done great things for them."

O Lord God of Israel, restore my fortunes, decorate my life, do good to me in Your good pleasure. Fill my mouth with laughter and let my tongue shout for joy. I earnestly ask for laughter; deep rooted, deep seated laughter, Lord I ask of You.

LET US PRAY

My times are in Your hands, cause my season of joy, chuckling, amusement, merriment, giggling, rejoicing, dancing, shouting and laughing to be now. Tune it on Father. Activate my laughter mode!

The Bible says in Proverbs 15:13,
> "A merry heart makes a cheerful countenance, But by sorrow of the heart the spirit is broken."

Also, Proverbs 17:22 says,
> "A merry heart does good, like medicine, But a broken spirit dries the bones."

Dear Lord, I pray my bones will not dry up. In Your mercy suffer me not with the sorrow of heart. Deal me with the medicine of merriment and sustain cheerful countenance in me.

Jeremiah 30:19a says,
> "Out of those places you will hear songs of thanksgiving and the sounds of laughter and merriment."

LET US PRAY

Almighty, all powerful Father, out of me, let there proceed sounds of laughter and merriment, with songs of thanksgiving in the name of Jesus Christ. Permit no sorrow to mingle with my joy. Though it is written in Proverbs 14:13,

> "Even in laughter the heart may ache, and the end of joy may be grief."

Lord, I forbid in the name above all names, the name of Jesus Christ, my laughter will not come with any form of heartache nor will my joy end in grief. I confess again and again Lord, "I shall Laugh, I shall Laugh, I shall Laugh in the name of Jesus Christ.

NOTES

TESTIMONY

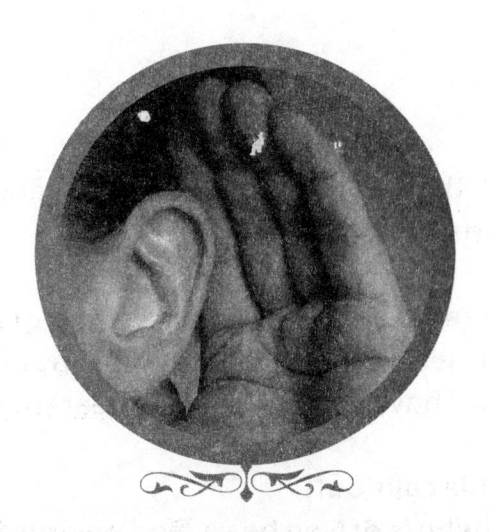

My Ears Will Hear You Lord

Heavenly Father I worship You. Isaiah 64:8 says,

> "...O LORD, You are our Father; We are the clay, and You our potter; And all we are the work of Your hand."

This o Lord is the wholesome truth. You formed and made me, You moulded me into Who You want and I am nothing without You. How great and awesome You are. I, the creation of Your hand choose to honour You my Potter.

The scripture says, in Jeremiah 18:2,
> "Arise and go down to the potter's house,

LET US PRAY
───────────

and there I will cause you to hear My words."

To this intent I come to You, the Potter of creation. With You is the life giving and life transforming word, and I have come that I may hear Your word.

John 8:47a calls out,
"He who is of God hears God's words."

As a fearfully and wonderfully created work of Your hand, You have given me ears and did not deny me of eyes. Your word clearly states,

"The hearing ear and the seeing eye, The LORD has made them both" [Proverbs 20:12].

The purpose of the ear is to hear, I therefore refuse the tragedy of dullness of heart and heaviness of ear in the name of Jesus. Unto some the Bible says,

"the Lord hath not given you an heart to perceive, and eyes to see, and ears to hear, unto this day." [Deuteronomy 29:4].

LET US PRAY

As You live my Father, this will not be my portion. I am not of them written in Psalms 115:6,

> "They have ears, but they hear not: noses have they, but they smell not:"

> Psalms 135:17
> "They have ears, but they do not hear; Nor is there any breath in their mouths."

Father, I will hear, and You O Lord alone will I hear.

As Psalms 85:8 says,
> "I will hear what God the Lord will speak: for he will speak peace unto his people, and to his saints…"

I refuse to be presumptuous; Your word will I hear and obey. When You speak I will hear. Deuteronomy 1:43 is not my case as it says,

> "So I spake unto you; and ye would not hear, but rebelled against the commandment of the Lord, and went presumptuously up into the hill."

LET US PRAY

Oh no, I refuse presumption.

Obadiah 1:3a says,
"Your presumptuous heart has deceived you."

My Father I choose a hearing ear and yielded heart of obedience.

Proverbs 1:5a says,
"A wise man will hear and increase learning."

Proverbs 8:33 says,
"Hear instruction and be wise, And do not disdain it."

Lord in the name of Jesus Christ, I pray my ears will hear you with clarity. Pride will not enter into me. I will hear as Jeremiah 13:15 admonishes,

"Hear and give ear: Do not be proud, For the LORD has spoken."

I reach out to You heavenly Father, let me hear You,

LET US PRAY

You that spoke to Moses from the midst of the bush and he heard you as it is written in Exodus 3:4b,

> "God called to him from the midst of the bush and said, "Moses, Moses!" And he said, "Here I am."

Lord, You also spoke to Elijah in the still small voice and caused him to hear You as recorded in I Kings 19:12-13,

> "and after the earthquake a fire, but the LORD was not in the fire; and after the fire a still small voice. So it was, when Elijah heard it, that he wrapped his face in his mantle and went out and stood in the entrance of the cave. Suddenly a voice came to him, and said, "What are you doing here, Elijah?"

Lord, You assured me in Isaiah 30:21 saying,

> "Your ears shall hear a word behind you, saying, "This is the way, walk in it,"

LET US PRAY

Whenever you turn to the right hand or whenever you turn to the left."

LORD, cause my ear to hear You as and when You speak. I need to hear from You, I want Your word O Lord; I am Your sheep. Your voice I must not miss.

The Bible says in John 10:27,
"My sheep hear My voice, and I know them, and they follow Me." Your voice I will hear my Father and my God, and in the name of Jesus Christ my heart will never be hardened to Your word; as it is written,

"Do not harden your hearts as in the rebellion, In the day of trial in the wilderness," [Hebrews 3:8].

Jehovah, let me hear from You in the name of Jesus Christ.

NOTES

TESTIMONY

I Shall Lack Nothing.

Eternal God, King of kings. Father of the less privileged, I AM THAT I AM, Yahweh Jireh, God of Abaraham's provision, as it is written in scriptures,

> "Abraham named the place Yahweh-Yireh (which means "the Lord will provide") Genesis 22:14.

To You I give all the praise. You, O Lord our Provider, to You I pray your word as written in Psalm 34:10 which says,

> "The young lions lack [food] and grow

hungry, But they who seek the LORD will not lack any good thing."

I pray in the name of Jesus Christ that under Your watch of me, I shall never lack any good thing.

Your word says,
"I will abundantly bless her provision; I will satisfy her poor with bread." [Psalms 132:15].

Deuteronomy 28:12b says,
"The LORD... bless all the work of your hand; and you will lend to many nations, but you will not borrow."

Father God, now bless abundantly as You have promised my provision and the work of my hands; satisfy me with Your bread.

I pray Psalm 144:13,
"That our barns may be full, supplying all kinds of produce; That our sheep may bring forth thousands and ten thousands in our fields."

LET US PRAY

As You blessed king Solomon with daily provision without fail, so Lord open up avenues of daily, weekly and monthly provision year in, year out, for the bible records the testimony of Solomon in I Kings 4:7,

> "And Solomon had twelve governors over all Israel, who provided food for the king and his household; each one made provision for one month of the year."

Father appoint "governors of provision" for me as You did for Solomon. Give command concerning me and allocate a settled provision to meet my needs and daily requirements in the name of Jesus Christ.

Nehemiah 11:23 says,
> "For there was a commandment from the king concerning them, and a settled provision for the singers, as everyday required."

As for the widow of Zarephath, her cruise never failed and her barrel of meal never wasted [not

LET US PRAY

even for a day], so Lord do unto me and more; let there be unending supply and provision of resources and all that my daily exigencies require.

> "Even the strong and the wealthy grow weak and hungry, but those who passionately pursue the Lord will never lack any good thing." [Psalms 34:10].

Standing on the strength of this word, I shall not lack any good thing. I put my trust in You Yahweh Jireh, that my portion is in Your word as written in Deuteronomy 8:7, 9,

> "For the Lord your God is bringing you into a good land of flowing streams and pools of water, with fountains and springs that gush out in the valleys and hills. It is a land where food is plentiful and nothing is lacking. It is a land where iron is as common as stone, and copper is abundant in the hills."

God, I thank You for my land of plenty where nothing good is lacking. My needs are well

LET US PRAY

provided for. The Bible says,

> "Whoever gives to the poor will lack nothing" [Proverbs 28:27].

Remember my giving to the poor and cause me to lack nothing that my destiny journey requires in the name of Jesus Christ.

I know Your word says,
> "...God is able to make all grace abound toward you, that you, always having all sufficiency in all things, may have an abundance for every good work." [II Corinthians 9:8].

Therefore my Father be it unto me according to Your word. Let Your grace abound towards me, let me have sufficiency in all good things. Open unto me Your treasure according to Deuteronomy 28:12,

> "The LORD will open to you His good treasure, the heavens, to give the rain to your land in its season, and to bless all

LET US PRAY

the work of your hand. You shall lend to many nations, but you shall not borrow."

Give rain to my land o Lord; bless me and cause me to become a lender to nations.

You said in Isaiah 41:18,
> "I will open rivers in desolate heights,
> And fountains in the midst of the valleys;
> I will make the wilderness a pool of water,
> and the dry land springs of water."

Father, do of Your good pleasure in my life. Make me a thousand times much more than my current size [materially, financially and in every sphere of need] in the name of Jesus Christ; for the bible says,

> "May the LORD God of your fathers make you a thousand times more numerous than you are, and bless you as He has promised you!" [Deuteronomy 1:11].

Bless me and mine as You have promised and let the earth yield its produce unto me, and let God,

LET US PRAY

even my God, bless me as is written in Psalms 67:6.

I thank You for I am assured by this prayer of Your unfailing provision and blessings in my life in the name of Jesus Christ. Amen

NOTES

TESTIMONY

Deliver Me, O Lord!

Mighty One in battle, Ancient of days, I give you honour. You are God and there is no other. Deuteronomy 32:39 quotes You saying,

> "Now see that I, even I, am He, And there is no God besides Me; I kill and I make alive; I wound and I heal; Nor is there any who can deliver from My hand."

Of a truth Father, no one can deliver from You; You are Jehovah Sabaoth - Man of War You are. I have come to magnify, glorify and praise You my God.

LET US PRAY

Psalms 140:13 says,
> "Your godly lovers will thank you no matter what happens. For they choose and cherish your presence above everything else!"

Your Presence is heaven to me. I thank You even as I realize I have no personal battles. Every attack of the evil one is not my battle but yours as it is written in II Chronicles 20:15c

> "...the battle is not yours, but God's."

I know that the warfare and pull that exist is not physical, for according to Ephesians 6:12b they are with the highest principalities and authorities operating in rebellion under the heavenly realms, For they are a powerful class of demon - gods and evil spirits that hold this dark world in bondage. Lord to this end, I also know by spiritual insight that

> "...the weapons of our warfare are not carnal, but mighty in God for pulling down strongholds," [II Corinthians 10:4].

LET US PRAY
───────────

I know that
> "The LORD does not save with sword and spear; for the battle is the LORD's" [I Samuel 17:47].

Your word says in II Kings 3:17a,
> "For thus says the LORD: 'You shall not see wind, nor shall you see rain; yet that valley shall be filled with water."

You are the mighty one Who certainly needs no weaponry to combat the enemy. Arise now Father and engage every enemy of my soul.

Job 5:19 says,
> "He shall deliver you in six troubles, Yes, in seven no evil shall touch you."

I am assured that You are my deliverer in every adverse situation. You will not leave me to myself because I am wrapped around by Your Presence. I am convinced that You my Lord will continue to deliver me from every form of evil and give me life. [2 Timothy 4:18a].

LET US PRAY

I pray now Father as Jesus taught in Luke 11:4c

"...deliver us from the evil one." Yes,

"Be pleased, O LORD, to deliver me; O LORD, make haste to help me! Let them be ashamed and brought to mutual confusion Who seek to destroy my life;" [Psalms 40:13-14a].

The Bible says,
"Like birds flying about, So will the LORD of hosts defend Jerusalem. Defending, He will also deliver it; Passing over, He will preserve it." [Isaiah 31:5].

Preserve me my Father. Preserve my household and everything that carries my signature. Arise to my defence, defend me mighty God.

"O LORD my God, in You I put my trust; Save me from all those who persecute me; And deliver me," [Psalms 7:1].

LET US PRAY

You said,
> "Call upon Me in the day of trouble; I will deliver you, and you shall glorify Me." [Psalms 50:15].

Even now o Lord, I glorify You. To You alone glory, honour and majesty belong. I call on You with every fibre in me

> "Deliver me, O LORD, from evil men; Preserve me from violent men," [Psalms 140:1].

> "Keep me, O LORD, from the hands of the wicked; Preserve me from violent men, Who have purposed to make my steps stumble." [Psalms 140:4];

> "Deliver Me from the sword, My precious life from the power of the dog." [Psalms 22:20];

> "Don't let the wicked triumph over me, but bring down their every strategy to subdue me..." [Psalms 140:8];

"Oh, let the wickedness of the wicked come to an end, But establish the just." [Psalms 7:9].

Jeremiah 1:19 says,
"They will fight against you, But they shall not prevail against you. For I am with you," says the LORD, "to deliver you."

Psalms 91:3 states,
"He will rescue you from every hidden trap of the enemy, and he will protect you from false accusation and any deadly curse."

Jeremiah 15:21 then assures,
"I will deliver you from the hand of the wicked, And I will redeem you from the grip of the terrible."

Halleuyah! So Lord I pray,
"Do not deliver me to the will of my adversaries; For false witnesses have risen against me, And such as breathe

out violence." [Psalms 27:12].

"I thank you for answering my prayer and giving me victory!" [Psalms 118:21]

NOTES

TESTIMONY

My Help Comes From the Lord

Eternal One, the Help of the helpless, blessed be Your Holy name. Looking out for help in the place where there is no help is mere frustration; therefore, wisdom informs that I turn to You because I am assured as the word says in Psalms 121:2,

> "My help comes from the Lord, who made heaven and earth!"

I realize that my true help and protection come only from the Lord, my Creator who made the heavens and the earth.

LET US PRAY

"For the same God who made everything, our Creator and our mighty maker, he himself is our helper and defender!" [Psalms 124:8].

Psalms 37:5 says,
"Commit everything you do to the Lord. Trust him, and he will help you."

Lord, I trust You absolutely! Therefore I have come to commit my ways to You; I call upon you for help, for You are a ready and responsive God to those who would seek You. When the nations sidetracked You, then You said:

"I was ready to respond, but no one asked for help. I was ready to be found, but no one was looking for me. I said, 'Here I am, here I am!' to a nation that did not call on my name."
[Isaiah 65:1 NLT].

Jehovah as for me,
"I look to the Lord for help. I wait confidently for God to save me, and my God will certainly hear me." [Micah 7:7].

LET US PRAY

I know You will hear me, because it is in You to help especially those who have come to terms with the inability of man to help himself. I cannot pull through all by myself dear Lord; for this reason, I humble myself and ask for Your most needed help on all fronts in my life.

Father Lord, like Daniel, I choose to pray asking You for help. Daniel 6:11 says "the officials went together to Daniel's house and found him praying and asking for God's help." I plead for help O Lord, even as Samuel did in 1 Samuel 7:9,

> "So Samuel pleaded with the Lord to help Israel, and the Lord answered him."

Dear God, please answer me as I cry for Your help. For it is written in Deuteronomy 33:26,

> "There is no one like the God of Israel. He rides across the heavens to help you, across the skies in majestic splendor."

Lord, ride across Your heavens. Come swiftly to help me in Your majestic splendor.

LET US PRAY

The Bible says in 2 Chronicles 25:8c,
> "for he has the power to help you or to trip you up."

Lord, let helping me be Your choice, do not trip me for hopelessness. Your help and wisdom is what I long for. God, I refuse to be in the shoes of those who receive no answer or help from You. Your word says in Psalms 18:41,

> "They called for help, but no one came to their rescue. They even cried to the Lord, but he refused to answer."

Ha! Lord God, I refuse abandonment, I will not be left alone to paddle the boat of my life in the name of Jesus Christ. Help me Lord, help me!

Your word says in Isaiah 30:19,
> "...you will weep no more. He will be gracious if you ask for help. He will surely respond to the sound of your cries."

Lord, make good Your word. Respond to my cry and plea for help, be gracious to me and help me.

LET US PRAY

"Listen to my cry for help, my King and my God, for I pray to no one but you." [Psalms 5:2].

My hope is in You as the scriptures says in Psalms 33:20,

> "We put our hope in the Lord. He is our help and our shield."

The Psalmist declared in Psalms 20:2,

> "May he send you help from his sanctuary and strengthen you from Jerusalem."

Father send me help. By Yourself you said in Isaiah 41:27,

> "Look! Help is on the way!' I will send Jerusalem a messenger with good news."

Also in Isaiah 41:10 & 13, You said,

LET US PRAY

> "Don't be afraid, for I am with you. Don't be discouraged, for I am your God. I will strengthen you and help you. I will hold you up with my victorious right hand. For I hold you by your right hand – I, the Lord your God. And I say to you, 'Don't be afraid. I am here to help you.'"

Thank You Lord for reassuring and encouraging my heart that You will help me. Father, I eagerly look forward to the messenger of good news, a helper whom You will send my way.

Father, Your word says in Judges 3:9,
> "But when the people of Israel cried out to the Lord for help, the Lord raised up a rescuer to save them. His name was Othniel, the son of Caleb's younger brother, Kenaz."

Raise me helpers in response to this fervent plea for help. I know You won't descend again in human form, You will only work by Your Holy Spirit moving men and women in place to do Your bidding in my life. Father, as You have done severally in the

LET US PRAY

scriptures, even in my life do it again as recorded in Numbers 34:18,

> "Enlist one leader from each tribe to help them with the task."

Deploy people, men and women of worth who will help me with every task I have been assigned on my destiny. I will not be stranded, nor overwhelmed in the name of Jesus Christ.

Lord, touch my helpers this day. They will not hold back nor slacken because You are the God that orchestrates godly things. Like the midwives refused to sabotage the delivery of the Hebrew children, so also raise helpers who will not be lured, manipulated or polluted on their mission to me. It is written in Exodus 1:16 & 17,

> "When you help the Hebrew women as they give birth, watch as they deliver. If the baby is a boy, kill him; if it is a girl, let her live." "But because the midwives feared God, they refused to obey the king's orders. They allowed the boys to live, too."

LET US PRAY

There will be no evil collaboration with my helpers of destiny in the mighty name of Jesus Christ.

Father, send me sold out, stop-at-nothing helpers who will do anything godly within their power to ensure that I get the help and assistance that I need per time. Abner being so resolute said,

> "May God strike me and even kill me if I don't do everything I can to help David get what the Lord has promised him!" [2 Samuel 3:9].

David pledged to Barzillai,

> "Kimham will go with me, and I will help him in any way you would like. And I will do for you anything you want." [2 Samuel 19:38].

Exodus 18:22b says,
> "They will help you carry the load, making the task easier for you."

Father, send me impactful helpers of destiny and by that make my work lighter and easier Jehovah.

LET US PRAY

Let it become so apparent that I found Your help. Nehemiah was a man helped by You and it was evident even to his enemies for he said in Nehemiah 6:16b,

> "They realized this work had been done with the help of our God."

Jehovah my Helper, do much for me. Help me evidently in the name of Jesus Christ.

Psalms 51:18 says
> "Look with favor on Zion and help her."

Let favour provoke Your help in every facet of my life; for I know that,

> "With God's help we will do mighty things" as stated in your word in Psalms 60:12a.

Thank You my Helper for answering me in the name of Jesus Christ I pray. Amen.

NOTES

TESTIMONY

Hear My Prayers Lord.

Almighty and Everlasting, Ever listening Father,

"I will praise you as long as I live, lifting up my hands to you in prayer." [Psalms 63:4].

You are most deserving of my praise and from the depth of my core I bring You the praise that is due Your Holy name. Be magnified dear God.

The scripture says in Psalm 65:2,
"You who answer prayer, to you all people will come.";

Therefore to You, the prayer answering God, I come.

LET US PRAY

"If I regard iniquity in my heart, The Lord will not hear." [Psalms 66:18] and

"if you measured us and marked us with our sins, who would ever have their prayers answered? But your forgiving love is what makes you so wonderful" [Psalms 130:3-4a].

My Father, I therefore confess my sins before you; I am deeply sorry for what I have done. The Bible says in 1 John 1:9,

"if we confess our sins to him, he is faithful and just to forgive us our sins and to cleanse us from all wickedness."

Mighty God, ever compassionate and forgiving, I ask that You cleanse and blot out all my fault and sin that can hinder You from hearing my prayer in the name of Jesus Christ. According to Psalms 39:12a, I say Lord please,

"Hear my prayer, O Lord! Listen to my cries for help! Don't ignore my tears. ...I am a man of prayer" [Psalm 109:4b],

LET US PRAY

"O Lord, hear me as I pray…" [Psalms 5:1a].

In Luke 11:1b the disciples said,
"…Lord, teach us to pray"

Father I ask as the disciples of Jesus did that as I pray, You Lord will teach me to pray. Your words says in Zechariah 12:10,

"I will pour out a spirit of grace and prayer"

My Father pour out on me the spirit of grace and supplication, that I may stand with unflinching tenacity in the place of prayer.

It is written concerning Christ,
"he spake a parable unto them to this end, that men ought always to pray, and not to faint" [Luke 18:1].

I refuse to faint. I choose Lord to pray as is comely to You. Your word enjoins me, "Make your life a prayer."

"Never stop praying. [1 Thessalonians 5:17].

LET US PRAY

Lord, I am resolute to pray! Hear me Lord when I pray; Jehovah,

> "Hear me, Lord, my plea is just; listen to my cry. Hear my prayer – it does not rise from deceitful lips." [Psalm 17:1].

The Bible says in Psalms 32:6,
> "Therefore, let all the godly pray to you while there is still time, that they may not drown in the flood waters of judgment."

Now is the set time to seek You my Lord.
> "Listen to my prayer, O God, do not ignore my plea; hear me and answer me..." [Psalm 55:1-2a].

In the name of Jesus, I come against every opposing spirit and all adversaries of prayer on a mission to withstand and resist my prayer. I forbid all such powers that withstood Daniel's answers as made known by the angel who said in Daniel 10:13a,

> "But the prince of the kingdom of Persia was standing in opposition to me for twenty-one days"

LET US PRAY
———————

I overcome powers, thrones, princes, in unseen realms by the blood of the lamb; for the book of Revelation says,

> "But they overcame him by the blood of the Lamb" [Revelation 12:11].

I conquer completely through the blood of the Lamb. I beseech You,

> "Lord, hear my voice! Let Your ears be attentive to the voice of my supplications.' [Psalms 130:2].

It is written,
> "Don't worry about anything; instead, pray about everything. Tell God what you need, and thank him for all he has done." [Philippians 4:6].

As I thank You for all that You have done, which are too innumerable to mention, Father I boldly bring up before You, everything [worries, concerns, burdens, anxieties, needs, challenges, restrictions, difficulties, battles, oppressions, attacks, strongholds, afflictions, bondages, stagnation, enchantments, divinations, stress,

LET US PRAY
―――――――――

fear, pain, dreams, visions, exploits, plans, pursuits, desires, and all things]. Oh God, I have come to lay them all down.

Your word says,
> "Are you weary, carrying a heavy burden? Then come to me. I will refresh your life, for I am your Oasis." [Matthew 11:28].

To You my Oasis I come, hear me, and answer. It is written,

> "For My yoke is easy [to bear] and My burden is light." [Matthew 11:30].

I therefore exchange every burden for Your yoke.

> "You answer us with awesome and righteous deeds, God our Savior, the hope of all the ends of the earth and of the farthest seas," [Psalm 65:5].

Going by scriptural accounts, when the godly pray, Father You answer; the Bible says

> "Then Jehoahaz prayed for the Lord's help, and the Lord heard his prayer..." [2 Kings 13:4];

LET US PRAY

"And the Lord listened to Hezekiah's prayer and healed the people." [2 Chronicles 30:20].

"When David saw that the Lord had answered his prayer, he offered sacrifices there at Araunah's threshing floor." [1 Chronicles 21:28].

Even Jesus had to pray and never for once failing in answers Jesus testified in John 11:42a, I know that you always answer my prayers. I passionately cry,

"Hear my prayer, O LORD, Give ear to my supplications! In Your faithfulness answer me" [Psalms 143:1].

"Give ear, O LORD, to my prayer; And attend to the voice of my supplications." [Psalms 86:6].

"Bend down, O Lord, and hear my prayer; answer me." [Psalms 86:1a].

"O Lord, hear me as I pray; pay attention to my groaning." [Psalms 5:1].

LET US PRAY

Father, I ask that Your Spirit will help me to channel my prayer appropriately; for it is written that

> "In the same way the Spirit [comes to us and] helps us in our weakness. We do not know what prayer to offer or how to offer it as we should, but the Spirit Himself [knows our need and at the right time] intercedes on our behalf with sighs and groanings too deep for words."
> [Romans 8:26].

Note: (If you are baptised in the Holy Spirit with evidence of speaking in tongues, allow the Spirit to speak up for you now. Pray in the Holy Spirit for an extended period).

Thank You Lord, thank You, thank You!

> "I thank you for answering my prayer and giving me victory!" [Psalms 118:21].

In the name of Jesus Christ I pray. Amen, Hallelujah!

NOTES

TESTIMONY

Lord, Remember Me This Day

Immortal, Invisible and Unchanging God. Omnipotent and Omniscient Lord. God of all creation, nothing fails Your memory. The Scripture says in Isaiah 49:15-16,

> "Can a woman forget her nursing child, And not have compassion on the son of her womb?" Surely they may forget, Yet I will not forget you. See, I have inscribed you on the palms of My hands; Your walls are continually before Me."

You O Lord never forget, You never forget the works of Your hand; especially man created in Your image and more importantly Your chosen ones.

LET US PRAY

It is written,

> "For God, the Faithful One, is not unfair. How can he forget the beautiful work you have done for him? He remembers the love you demonstrate as you continually serve his beloved ones for the glory of his name." [Hebrews 6:10].

What a faithful God You are. To the details of my works You take note of Lord. Your word says,

> "The very hairs of your head are all numbered." "So don't worry. For your Father cares deeply about even the smallest detail of your life."
> [Matthew 10:30-31].

Such a joy to know You have my details and Your system cannot shut down on me. I give You glory and praise Jehovah.

> "Wake up! Rise to my defense! Take up my case, my God and my Lord."
> [Psalms 35:23].

LET US PRAY

"Do not keep silent, O God; Do not hold Your peace or be still, O God." [Psalm 83:1].

Be stirred up to bless me O Lord. The Bible records the stirring of Ahaserus that kept him awake all because of Mordecai. David was also stirred up because of Mephibosheth in II Samuel 9:3-5, 7. Lord for the sake of Joseph, Pharaoh was stirred up by a need to understand a dream. I know my Father, You are not man that will change Your mind, yet this day I call for a book of remembrance to be opened on my account.

"Remember your promise to me;
it is my only hope." [Psalms 119:49].

Father, remember me for good. It is written

"Every good thing given and every perfect gift is from above; it comes down from the Father of lights [the Creator and Sustainer of the heavens], in whom there is no variation [no rising or setting] or shadow cast by His turning [for He is perfect and never changes." [James 1:17].

LET US PRAY

And I know You do not refuse any good thing to those who do what is right. Though I have no right standing in myself, yet

> "I now have the righteousness that is given through faith in Christ." [Philippians 3:9b].

The Bible says in Romans 8:32,
> "Since he did not spare even his own Son but gave him up for us all, won't he also give us everything else?"

I am assured Father that nothing due to me in You shall be restrained or held back from me.

> "Come quickly to help me, O Lord my savior." [Psalms 38:22].

Remember me, O my God, for good [Nehemiah 13:31c]. It is written that you reward those who earnestly and diligently seek you. Like Hezekiah, I turn to You,

LET US PRAY

> "Remember, Lord, how I have walked before you faithfully and with wholehearted devotion and have done what is good in your eyes." [Isaiah 38:3].

As the Psalmist prayed in Psalms 20:3,

> "May he remember all your gifts and look favorably on your burnt offerings. Lord remember me, remember my gifts, remember my seeds, remember my sacrifices."

Father remember! Like Nehemiah, I cry to You as He did in your word,

> "Remember me with favor, my God, for all I have done for these people." Nehemiah 5:19.

Nehemiah 13:22 says,
> "Remember this good deed also, O my God! Have compassion on me according to your great and unfailing love."

LET US PRAY

Nehemiah 13:14,

    "Remember me, O my God, concerning this, and do not wipe out my good deeds that I have done for the house of my God, and for its services!"

In Your goodness,

    "Remember me and visit me; "Lord, you understand; remember me and care for me" [Jeremiah 15:15].

I press in,

    "Remember, Lord, your great mercy and love, for they are from of old…according to your love remember me, for you, Lord, are good." [Psalm 25:6-7b]

"Remember me, Lord, when you show favor to your people, come to my aid when you save them, that I may enjoy the prosperity of your chosen ones, that I may share in the joy of your nation and join your inheritance in giving praise." [Psalm 106:4-5].

LET US PRAY

I bless Your name Jehovah for I know I am remembered. I will not hold back in telling of Your goodness, as I enjoy the fatness of Your blessings. Thank You Ancient of days. In the mighty name of Jesus Christ I pray. Amen.

NOTES

TESTIMONY

Let There Be Light!

Father, the One of Whom the scriptures says in 1 John 1:5 that

> "God is light, and in him is no darkness at all."

Truly there is no iota of darkness that can penetrate You ever. John 1:5 records that,

> "The light shines in the darkness, and the darkness hasn't overcome it."

You, my dear Lord are the One in 2 Corinthians 4:6a who said,

LET US PRAY

"Let light shine out of darkness"

I bring my life to Your Light, Father make Your Light shine in my heart. Let Your Light kindle light in me. Shine down Your Light on me, in Your Presence darkness flees, for no darkness can comprehend light.

The Bible says in Matthew 5:14,
>"You are the light of the world - like a city on a hilltop that cannot be hidden."

I confess as it is scripted of me by You, "I am the light of the world". The main characteristic of light is to shine.

Matthew 5:15 says
>"No one lights a lamp and then puts it under a basket. Instead, a lamp is placed on a stand, where it gives light to everyone in the house."

I ask vehemently now, for a change of position. Relocate me dear Lord to the 'stand' of life that you have prepared for me, where I can give light to

LET US PRAY

others. Lord, as the bible says in Psalm 40:2,

> "He brought me up also out of a horrible pit, out of the miry clay. He set my feet on a rock, and gave me a firm place to stand."

Position me Father upon the heights even as it is written in Psalm 18:33,

> "He makes my feet like the feet of a deer; he causes me to stand on the heights."

I refuse to be hidden under the bushel, my light will not be dull nor do I succumb to irrelevance in the name of Jesus Christ. I am destined to shine as light, therefore I arise and I choose to shine as commanded in Isaiah 60:1,

> "Arise, shine; for your light has come, and the Lord's glory has risen on you."

My Father, let Your glory fall on me.

> Psalms 18:28 says,
> "For you will light my lamp, Yahweh. My

LET US PRAY

God will light up my darkness."

My shining as light is orchestrated by You, so Father cause my light to shine.

Isaiah 60:19 says,
> "The sun will no more be your light by day, nor will the brightness of the moon shine on you, for the Lord will be your everlasting light, and your God will be your glory."

Jehovah, You are my everlasting and unquenchable Light. Let my light so shine before men O Lord, let me not live my days in darkness. Cause my good deeds to be seen. I forbid darkness. I will not be hidden, my works will not be hidden, my impact shall be felt, I am visible in the mighty name of Jesus Christ.

Jesus said in John 12:46,
> "I have come into the world as a Light, so that no one who believes in me should stay in darkness."

LET US PRAY
———

I believe in Jesus, I believe that He came, I believe He died on the cross and rose again; I believe absolutely in Jesus and His saving power. I am saved, I am a believer, therefore I will never live in the dark.

Job 29:3 says,
> "when his lamp shone on my head and by his light I walked through darkness!"

Through the Light of Christ in Whom I believe, I walk through every seeming darkness surrounding my life. I stand up against every darkness from the pit of hell. I penetrate, piercing and shining through every dark cloud; waging war against every generator and source of darkness in and around me. I carry light, I am light, and I shine my light as the Lord God Almighty lives.

On the account of the strength of the Light who is the source of my light, my testimony becomes like that of Job's in Job 29:8-10,

> "The young men would see me and step aside, and the old men would get up and remain standing; the chief men

LET US PRAY
_____

refrained from talking and covered their mouths with their hands; the voices of the nobles fell silent, and their tongues stuck to the roof of their mouths."

The Bible says in Ephesians 5:14a,
 "For everything made evident is light"

Father in the name of Jesus Christ, make me evident as the light that I truly am. Let my life count, let me shine in the name of Jesus Christ I pray. Amen.

NOTES

TESTIMONY

Grant Me Success Oh Lord!

Eternal God, Who does not fail, You are the God in and with Whom all things are possible; for the Bible says in Mark 10:27,

> "Jesus looked at them and replied, "This is impossible for mere humans, but not for God; all things are possible for God."

Lord, with You lies possibilities. I pray that every attempt of progress that I have failed at on my life's journey be revisited in Your infinite mercy in the name of Jesus Christ. Make impossibilities become possible for me henceforth. Eleazar, Abraham's servant, prayed saying,

LET US PRAY

"Lord, God of my master Abraham, make me successful today, and show kindness to my master Abraham." [Genesis 24:12].

Lord you granted him just as he had prayed.

Psalm 20:4 says,
> "May he grant your heart's desires and make all your plans succeed."

Almighty Father, I pray, grant me my heart desires and cause my plans to succeed in life become a tangible reality. Help me Lord to succeed. You helped David, help me too dear Lord. According to 1 Samuel 18:14,

> "Now David achieved success in all he did, for the LORD was with him."

David's success was clearly on Your account, Jehovah, please be with me and give me success in all my undertakings in the mighty name of Jesus Christ.

LET US PRAY

Job 22:28 says,
"You will succeed in whatever you choose to do, and light will shine on the road ahead of you.";

Lord, let Your light shine on the road of my destiny and let all I am scripted to do succeed at Your watch. I pray into my life now that I will have good success in both Your eyes O God and that of men.

Proverbs 3:4 says,
"So you will find favor and good success in the sight of God and man."

The Bible says,
"It is he who blesses you with bountiful harvests and gives you success in all your work. This festival will be a time of great joy for all." [Deuteronomy 16:15].

Almighty God, please give me success in all my work and let my joy be full. I refuse to stall, I choose success, and I will succeed in the name of Jesus Christ.

LET US PRAY

It is written concerning king Uzziah that he, "sought God during the days of Zechariah, who taught him to fear God. And as long as the king sought guidance from the Lord, God gave him success." [2 Chronicles 26:5].

My God, I seek Your guidance, please do not leave me to myself. Psalm 25:5 says,

> "Guide me in your truth and teach me, for you are God my Savior, and my hope is in you all day long."

Jehovah, guide me and give me success indeed. Bring me to the discovery of wisdom which is the fount of success. The Bible says in Proverbs 8:14a,

> "You will find true success when you find me, for I have insight into wise plans that are designed just for you."

The scripture says,
> "If the ax is dull and its edge unsharpened, more strength is needed,

LET US PRAY

but skill will bring success." [Ecclesiastes 10:10].

O Lord, let me into wisdom, skill me up by Your wisdom, as You bestowed on David, for it is written,

> "On every mission on which Saul sent him, David achieved success."
> [1 Samuel 18:5].

I refuse to fail on any mission I set out to do. No hold to my success, no delay to my success for Eleazar said,

> "Don't detain me – the LORD has granted me success on my journey."
> [Genesis 24:56].

Father, thank You for granting me success even as I have asked in the mighty name of Jesus Christ. Amen.

NOTES

TESTIMONY

Give Me Your Understanding Lord!

My Father and my God, how great You are. Your power is absolute and Your understanding is beyond comprehension. Psalms 147:5 declares

> "How great is our Lord! His power is absolute! His understanding is beyond comprehension!"

Jehovah, my hunger and thirst is to tap from Your incomprehensible depth of understanding. Your only begotten Son, Jesus Christ, when He was on this side of eternity, understanding was one of His distinguishing graces. Luke 2:47 says,

LET US PRAY

"All who heard him were amazed at his understanding and his answers."

Lord bless me now with an amazing depth of understanding. The Bible says,

> "Senseless people do not know, fools do not understand." [Psalm 92:6].

My God, I refuse to be senseless, thoughtless or foolish. I am Your servant, please give understanding as it is written in Psalm 119:125,

> "I am your servant; give me discernment that I may understand your statutes."

I truly want to understand You, Your word and Your very will for my life par time. You sent Your angel to aid Daniel by giving him understanding, for the angel said in Daniel 9:22,

> "Daniel, I have come here to give you insight and understanding."

O Lord my God, same yesterday, today and

LET US PRAY

forever, please give me insight and understanding. Teach me what I ought to know, give me grace to dissect and comprehend what it is that You are teaching and saying to me. I do not want to be ignorant, or a know-nothing moron, or a numbskull on the path of destiny. Father, give me understanding. As each day dawns, do as it is written in Isaiah 50:4,

> "Morning by morning he wakens me and opens my understanding to his will."

Open my understanding to Your will my God. I refuse to be a blockhead, give me understanding.

Luke 24:45 says,
> "Then he opened their minds to understand the Scriptures."

Open my mind to understanding Your scriptures. Let the word be more than mere letters to me. Give me great understanding. Do not let Your word appear to me as parables Father, give me understanding. Give clarity when You speak to me Lord. Help me to understand situations and

LET US PRAY

circumstances. I refuse to grope in darkness my Lord. Give me an understanding heart. [1 Kings 3:9]. You gave Solomon when he asked of You, Father give me also just as You gave him an understanding heart for You are no respecter of persons.

The Bible says,
> "The farmer knows just what to do, for God has given him understanding." [Isaiah 28:26].

If You gave the farmer understanding of his task, Father give me understanding of every detail of each facet of my life. Let my portion be a clear manifestation of Your word in Isaiah 11:2a which says,

> "And the Spirit of the Lord will rest on him - the Spirit of wisdom and understanding."

Your word says,
> "Fools have no interest in understanding; they only want to air their own opinions." [Proverbs 18:2].

LET US PRAY

Jehovah I scream it out, "I want understanding"! I refuse to walk the path of fools.

Proverbs 19:8 records,
>"People who cherish understanding will prosper."

Father, cause me to prosper for I cherish understanding. Let not Your understanding ever depart from me; by Your grace I mount up in understanding and my reigning is thereby established and sustained in the name of Jesus Christ. Amen.

NOTES

TESTIMONY

Joy Unlimited!

All exuberant God, You are most deserving of glory and honour. You are my very source of joy hence I come to draw from You joy. The Scriptures says in Psalm 126:5,

> "Those who sow in tears shall reap in joy."

Jehovah I have come to ask for joy, for the joy from You is my strength. My heart, O God, steadfastly latches on to You, therefore let joy shine down on me according to Your word in Psalms 97:11,

> "Light shines on the godly, and joy on those whose hearts are right."

LET US PRAY
———————

Father, fill me up with joy, for I have a right standing with You in Christ Jesus. Like the scripture says in Esther 8:16,

> "The Jews were filled with joy and gladness and were honored everywhere."

My Father, fill me with joy I pray.

You are the One that I adore, and my praise is ever due to You. In Your Presence is fullness of joy, so Lord,

> "Fill me with joy in your presence, with eternal pleasures at your right hand." [Psalm 16:11].

Psalms 28:7 says,
> "The Lord is my strength and shield. I trust him with all my heart. He helps me, and my heart is filled with joy. I burst out in songs of thanksgiving."

You are my strength Lord, I reaffirm again that You are my backbone and support; I have absolute

LET US PRAY
―――――――――

and unwavering confidence in You. Help me Lord, fill my heart with Joy. This is my desperate desire.

Sweet Holy Spirit, produce in me Your fruit. I remain a good soil for the fruit of the Spirit. Birth in me the Spirit of joy for the Bible says in Galatians 5:22,

> "The Holy Spirit produces this kind of fruit in our lives: love, joy, peace, patience, kindness, goodness, faithfulness."

I humble myself before You, I empty myself of every loftiness for it is written,

> "The humble also shall increase their joy in the LORD, And the poor among men shall rejoice In the Holy One of Israel." [Isaiah 29:19].

Increase my joy quotient. The Bible says,

> "You will live in joy and peace. The mountains and hills will burst into song, and the trees of the field will clap their hands! [Isaiah 55:12].

LET US PRAY

My joy comes now O God, fill me with joy. As I ask of You my Lord, do to me of Your good pleasure for it is written,

> "I will bring them to my holy mountain of Jerusalem and will fill them with joy in my house of prayer." [Isaiah 56:7].

God, land me on Your holy mountain, Your house of prayer, and fill me up Lord with joy. Mighty God, cause songs of joy to be heard like never before in my tabernacle. Psalms 118:15,

> "Songs of joy and victory are sung in the camp of the godly. The strong right arm of the Lord has done glorious things!"

You said:
> "I will make you beautiful forever, a joy to all generations." [Isaiah 60:15].

Lord, make me that joy that cuts across generations. Let my household and I say

LET US PRAY

"Jehovah hath done great things for us; and we are joyful." [Psalms 126:3].

Father, thank You for filling me with joy; no evil shall mess up with my Joy in the name of Jesus Christ.

NOTES

TESTIMONY

A New Heart, A New Spirit!

God of power and might, I bow before You in absolute surrender and worship. I honour You Jehovah God. Psalms 33:15 says about You,

> "He is the one who forms every human heart, and takes note of all their actions."

No one existing formed their heart, but You O God formed each one. Satan is the polluter of men's heart, for the Bible says in Jeremiah 17:9,

> "The heart is deceitful above all things, And desperately wicked; Who can know it?"

LET US PRAY

Wickedness takes the heart over, to this end O Lord, I come to You for cleansing. Scripture says,

> "Cleanse your heart and stop being so stubborn!" [Deuteronomy 10:16].

Dear God, in Deuteronomy 30:6a Your word says,

> "The LORD your God will also cleanse your heart."

> Father "Create for me a pure heart, O God! Renew a resolute spirit within me!" [Psalms 51:10].

I refuse to be like Pharaoh whose heart remained hardened according to Exodus 7:13a which says

> "Pharaoh's heart, however, remained hard."

Proverbs 28:14 says,
> "Blessed is the one who is always cautious, but whoever hardens his heart will fall into evil."

LET US PRAY

Father, I take caution, I soft pedal in my heart, my heart is yielded and submitted to You; I denounce every pride of heart and haughtiness and I pray in the name of Jesus Christ, my heart will not fall into evil. I bring my heart to You as I believe Your word in Ezekiel 36:26 that says,

> "I will give you a new heart and put a new spirit within you; I will take the heart of stone out of your flesh and give you a heart of flesh."

Lord, in Your mercy I ask that You take out of me every stony heart, every stubbornness, every presumption and sin my heart might have haboured. Give me a new heart, yielded and willing, tuned in to Your frequency alone. Proverbs 21:1 says,

> "The king's heart is in the hand of the LORD like channels of water; he turns it wherever he wants."

Jehovah, turn my heart wherever is pleasing to You per time. Program my heart to doing Your will

LET US PRAY
―――――

alone. Let nothing outside of You entice my heart. I chose to "Guard my heart above all else... "even as it is written in Proverbs 4:23.

I take my stand to store Your word in my heart as a guard against every evil penetration into my heart. O Lord, here is my resolve and prayer,

> "With all my heart I seek you. Do not allow me to stray from your commands! In my heart I store up your words, so I might not sin against you."
> [Psalms 119:10-11].

From this point of prayer dear Lord, I receive grace to be unto You as David; for in Acts 13:22, you testified of him,

> "I have found David the son of Jesse, a man after My own heart, who will do all My will.'"

Father, my heart pants after You even as the deer pants for the waters. I choose to do Your will, O God. As it is written in Psalms 57:7a,

LET US PRAY

"My heart is steadfast, O God, my heart is steadfast"

No pollution shall enter my heart in the name of Jesus Christ.

Jeremiah 17:10 says,
"I the Lord search the heart and examine the mind, to reward each person according to their conduct, according to what their deeds deserve."

Please Lord, preserve me in purity of heart and reward me accordingly in the name of Jesus Christ. Amen.

NOTES

TESTIMONY

Peace!

Jehovah Shalom, My Lord Who is peace, to you I come. It is written in Judges 6:24 that,

> "Gideon built an altar there to the LORD, and called it The-LORD-Is-Peace."

Indeed, You are the Lord of Peace and in reverence I acknowledge you this day.

Isaiah 53:5 says Your Son,
> "Was wounded for our transgressions, He was bruised for our iniquities; the chastisement for our peace was upon Him."

LET US PRAY

Thank You Jesus for paying the price for my peace way ahead. I declare that Your sacrifice shall never be in vain, and this day I choose and embrace Your peace. Leviticus 26:6 says,

> "I will give peace in the land, and you shall lie down, and none will make you afraid; I will rid the land of evil beasts, and the sword will not go through your land."

Mighty One, I make a demand on Your promise, give me peace, give my home peace, give my work peace, give my land peace in the name of Jesus Christ Who paid my price of access to this dimension of peace in You. Father, cause me and my entire household to lie down in peace without any form or appearance of fear in our lives.

Job 5:24 says,
> "You shall know that your tent is in peace; You shall visit your dwelling and find nothing amiss."

My God, let this be my reality. Let nothing be

LET US PRAY
───────

found amiss in my dwelling, let my territory be at peace in the name of Jesus Christ. The bible says in Psalms 147:14,

> "He makes peace in your borders, And fills you with the finest wheat."

Lord I pray vehemently for peace within my sphere. Let Your peace take over in every space I appear or occupy. Honour the script in Psalm 122:7 that says,

> "May peace be within your walls And prosperity within your palaces."

in the name of Jesus Christ. Only You Lord can give peace even as

> "Joseph answered Pharaoh, saying, " It is not in me; God will give Pharaoh an answer of peace."" [Genesis 41:16].

I therefore press asking You and You alone, it is not in any man to give me peace, Father establish Your peace in me.

LET US PRAY

Isaiah 26:12 says,
> "Lord, You will establish peace for us, For You have also done all our works in us."

Establish your peace O Lord.

Numbers 25:12 says,
> "I am making my special covenant of peace with him."

Thank You Father, for You do not break Your covenant nor alter Your words. Do to me Jehovah Shalom, according to Your word in Isaiah 26:3,

> "You will keep him in perfect peace, Whose mind is stayed on You, Because he trusts in You."

My mind is fixated on You my Father and God. Lord please keep me in perfect peace, permit nothing and no one to rattle my peace. Make a reality in my life Philippians 4:7,

> "And the peace of God, which surpasses all understanding, will guard your hearts and minds through Christ Jesus."

LET US PRAY
_____

Let my peace remain a mystery to all men.

I disallow terror, trouble, attack, panic, outbreak, sickness, lack, misunderstandings, quarrels, and everything that can spell unrest in my territory and life in the name of Jesus Christ. The Bible says in Mark 4:39,

> "Then He arose and rebuked the wind, and said to the sea, "Peace, be still!" And the wind ceased and there was a great calm."

Jesus let my atmosphere be agog with Your peace, still every storm.

I Kings 4:24 says,
> "...he had dominion over all the region on this side of the River from Tiphsah even to Gaza, namely over all the kings on this side of the River; and he had peace on every side all around him."

Jehovah grant me peace on all fronts. Your words states in Isaiah 66:12a,

LET US PRAY

"For thus says the LORD: "Behold, I will extend peace to her like a river."

Lord, flow Your peace into every area of my life. Let Your peace flow to me like a river flows with clean and fresh water. In all that you have permitted me across board, Father I speak Your peace in the name of Jesus Christ.

Almighty God, lift Your countenance upon my household and all that concerns me, give me peace as it is written in Numbers 6:26,

"LORD lift up His countenance upon you, and give you peace."

Proverbs 16:7 says,
"When a man's ways please the LORD,
He makes even his enemies to be at peace with him."

Jehovah, let my decisions and attending actions be pleasing to You, cause even those enraged against me for no cause, cease fire; Father activate peace between us. Bible says,

LET US PRAY

"Great peace have those who love Your law, And nothing causes them to stumble." [Psalms 119:165]

Isaiah 54:13 says "All your children shall be taught by the LORD, And great shall be the peace of your children."

Dear Lord, mega peace is all I am asking for. Peace without a loophole, grant to me now in the name of Jesus Christ. Jeremiah 29:11 declares

"I know the thoughts that I think toward you, says the LORD, thoughts of peace and not of evil, to give you a future and a hope."

Manifest Your peaceful thoughts in my life, that it might become a reality to the glory and praise of Your name my God. It is written in II Thessalonians 3:16

"Now may the Lord of peace Himself give you peace always in every way."

I declare in my life Shalom! Shalom! Shalom!

NOTES

TESTIMONY

No Anxiety

Eternal Rock of Ages, my God in Whom there is no variableness. You are an all-time solution provider, You never fail. I honor You for Who You are. Who You are brings me to You with all the baggages life has thrusted at me.

David, the great king after your heart fell prey of that which I also find myself; in Psalm 102:5 he said,

> "Because of the anxiety that makes me groan, my bones protrude from my skin."

In 2 Samuel 24:14a, he also said,
 "I have great anxieties."

LET US PRAY

In Psalm 38:8, the Psalmist yet says,
"I am numb with pain and severely battered; I groan loudly because of the anxiety I feel."

Paul said,
"Besides those things that are without, there is that which presseth upon me daily, anxiety for all the churches."
[2 Corinthians 11:28].

Father, though Jesus said in Matthew 6:34,

"Do not be anxious about tomorrow, for tomorrow will be anxious for itself. Let the day's own trouble be sufficient for the day";

yet, I confess that anxious thoughts render me numb and feeble. Proverbs 12:25a aptly expresses my disposition Lord,

"Anxiety in a man's heart weighs it down."

LET US PRAY

I come to You seeking the good and encouraging word that will gladden my heart even as Proverbs 12:25b recommends.

I have come to do as it is written in 1 Peter 5:7,

> "Cast all your anxiety on him because he cares for you."

Lord I know You care for me, Father let the anxieties in my heart be banished as Solomon had said in Ecclesiastes 11:10a,

> "So then, banish anxiety from your heart and cast off the troubles of your body."

Let all my troubles be gone, O God that answers prayers.

In 2 Samuel 24:14,
> "David answered Gad, "I have great anxiety. Please, let us fall into the Lord's hands because his mercies are great, but don't let me fall into human hands."

LET US PRAY

I am therefore walking in David's steps, I have come to fall into Your hands that I might find grace to overcome every nagging anxiety in me. I know my anxieties and worries cannot add anything good to my life nor can it elongate my days on this side of eternity, for Jesus had said in Matthew 6:27,

> "And which of you by being anxious can add one cubit to his span of life?"

Lord, I humble myself before You and I surrender all of my concerns to You here and now in the place of prayer. Scriptures says in Philippians 4:6,

> "Do not be anxious about anything, but in everything by prayer and supplication with thanksgiving let your requests be made known to God."

I intentionally give You thanks Lord, even as I trust You that the nagging thoughts, worries, anxieties, fears will be vamped out by Your mercy bestowed on me. I know You are bigger than all the cares of this world, I choose not to be anxious about anything any longer. I thank You for I know that You will give me relief from anxiety even as Isaiah assures,

> "When the LORD gives you relief from your suffering and anxiety, and from the hard labor which you were made to perform," [Isaiah 14:3].

Thank You Father for my liberty. I am free from anxiety in the name of Jesus Christ.

NOTES

TESTIMONY

Turn the Wicked Back to You Lord

Heavenly Father, Creator of the universe, God of Abraham, Isaac and Jacob, true and upright are You. Defender of the helpless is Who You are. I praise You according to Your righteousness even as David said in Psalm 7:17. You are the Just God of all times. Psalms 7:11 says,

> "God is a just judge, And God is angry with the wicked every day."

You hate wickedness and the way of the wicked is an abomination to you as it is written in Proverbs 15:9,

LET US PRAY

"The way of the wicked is an abomination to the LORD, But He loves him who follows righteousness."

The scriptures says,
"The heart is deceitful above all things, And desperately wicked; Who can know it?" [Jeremiah 17:9].

Father You alone detect even the wickedness that yet lies in the hearts of men unexpressed; because You said in Your word,

"I, the LORD, search the heart, I test the mind, Even to give every man according to his ways, According to the fruit of his doings." [Jeremiah 17:10];

though You yet ask in Ezekiel 18:23,

"Do I have any pleasure at all that the wicked should die?" says the Lord GOD, " and not that he should turn from his ways and live?"

LET US PRAY
———————

It is not Your good pleasure to destroy the wicked, for Your word says in Isaiah 55:7,

> "Let the wicked leave (behind) his way And the unrighteous man his thoughts; And let him return to the LORD, And He will have compassion (mercy) on him, And to our God, For He will abundantly pardon."

Ezekiel 18:21-22 says,
> "But if a wicked man turns from all his sins which he has committed, keeps all My statutes, and does what is lawful and right, he shall surely live; he shall not die. None of the transgressions which he has committed shall be remembered against him; because of the righteousness which he has done, he shall live."

I pray in accordance with Your desire that every wicked one will repent. Father, touch their heart this moment for repentance. Melt out the evil entrenched in their hearts so they can repent of

LET US PRAY

the stupor of wickedness and evil. Let the light of Christ shine to them and let them come to a true saving knowledge of Christ. Let the essence of the death and resurrection of Christ be enforced in their lives in the name of Jesus Christ.

It is written,
> "Who is a God like You, Pardoning iniquity And passing over the transgression of the remnant of His heritage? He does not retain His anger forever, Because He delights in mercy." [Micah 7:18].

Let the abundance of Your mercy avail over the wicked O dear God. Bring O God, to bear Your word, over anyone whose heart is pregnant with wickedness and anyone whose hand is soiled with evil. It is written,

> "But to him who does not work but believes on Him who justifies the ungodly, his faith is accounted for righteousness, just as David also describes the blessedness of the man to

LET US PRAY

whom God imputes righteousness apart from works: "Blessed are those whose lawless deeds are forgiven, And whose sins are covered; Blessed is the man to whom the LORD shall not impute sin."" [Romans 4:5-8]

Father God, please turn the hearts of the wicked to suddenly trust in You. As the light will shine their way by Your divine means, let them see their vomit with a dissatisfaction hence seek cleanness from Your Son, Jesus Christ. Father, let them have faith in You, and let righteousness be imputed to these ones even by Christ Jesus.

Merciful and loving Father, like Abraham,

> "Indeed now, I who am but dust and ashes have taken it upon myself to speak to the Lord." [Genesis 18:27],

please give heed to this prayer as I intercede for every wicked heart and evil hands; that they may come to true saving knowledge and experience the salvation in the name of Jesus Christ. Amen!

NOTES

TESTIMONY

Arise to my Defense O God!

Everlasting Father, God of all flesh; the Most High God that rules in the affairs of men. Honour and Majesty are Yours. The Lord of Sabaoth, God of the Angel armies Who fought the battle of the children of Israel,

> "O LORD my God, in You I put my trust; Save me from all those who persecute me; And deliver me, Lest they tear me like a lion, Rending me in pieces, while there is none to deliver." [Psalms 7:1-2].

Arise to my defence O God, deliver me from those who breathe cruelty. I know the scripture says,

LET US PRAY

> "The LORD is slow to anger and great in power, And will not at all acquit the wicked. The LORD has His way In the whirlwind and in the storm, And the clouds are the dust of His feet." [Nahum 1:3].

Therefore Father, do not acquit the wicked who have incessantly refused to repent of his evil ways and acts. I know You Father as a just God; and the Bible also says,

> "To turn aside the right of a man before the face of the most High, To subvert a man in his cause, the Lord approveth not." [Lamentations 3:35-36].

Give no permission to the wicked in my life, give them no foothold any longer. Jehovah, I beseech You,

> "Do not let those gloat over me who are my enemies without cause; do not let those who hate me without reason maliciously wink the eye." [Psalm 35:19].

LET US PRAY
———————

> "Give me not up to the will of my adversaries; for false witnesses have risen against me, and they breathe out violence." [Psalms 27:12].

> "For you are not a God who delights in wickedness; evil may not dwell with you." [Psalms 5:4].

The Bible says concerning You, O Lord,

> "For his eyes are on the ways of a man, and he sees all his steps. There is no gloom or deep darkness where evildoers may hide themselves. Thus, knowing their works, he overturns them in the night, and they are crushed. He strikes them for their wickedness in a place for all to see," [Job 34:21-22, 25-26].

My Lord and my God, help of the helpless, overturn every plot and scheme of the wicked which they devise against me; for it is written,

> "Hide me from the secret plots of the wicked, From the rebellion of the workers

LET US PRAY

of iniquity." [Psalms 64:2].
"Behold, the wicked brings forth iniquity; Yes, he conceives trouble and brings forth falsehood." [Psalms 7:14].

Scatter their ploy Jehovah. Your word assures me in Jeremiah 15:21,

"I will deliver you from the hand of the wicked, And I will redeem you from the grip of the terrible."

"Arise, O LORD, confront him, cast him down; Deliver my life from the wicked with Your sword," [Psalms 17:13].

"Keep me, O LORD, from the hands of the wicked; Preserve me from violent men, who have purposed to make my steps stumble." [Psalms 140:4].

"Break the power of the wicked and all their strong-arm tactics. Search them out and destroy them for the evil things they've done." [Psalms 10:15].

LET US PRAY
―――――――

"Oh, let the wickedness of the wicked come to an end." [Psalms 7:9a].

I refuse to stumble, I will not stumble, my foot will not slip, I will not get off track from You my God.

"Those who trust in the Lord are like Mount Zion, which cannot be shaken but endures forever." [Psalm 125:1].

Now Lord, please remember that,

"the scepter of wickedness shall not rest on the land allotted to the righteous, lest the righteous stretch out their hands to do wrong." [Psalms 125:3].

So I ask,
"Do not incline my heart to any evil thing, To practice wicked works with men who work iniquity; And do not let me eat of their delicacies." [Psalms 141:4].

For Your word says,
"You therefore, beloved, since you know

LET US PRAY

this beforehand, beware lest you also fall from your own steadfastness, being led away with the error of the wicked." [II Peter 3:17].

God I receive grace, I hide under Your covering, and I embrace Your Spirit. I refuse to be led away and lured into wickedness under any circumstance. My hand will not be soiled with the same error of evil.

> "Keep me as the apple of your eye; hide me in the shadow of your wings" [Psalm 17:8].

Your word says,
> "The enemy shall not outwit him, Nor the son of wickedness afflict him. I will beat down his foes before his face, And plague those who hate him. "But My faithfulness and My mercy shall be with him, And in My name his horn shall be exalted." [Psalms 89:22-24].

TESTIMONY

Commitment to Serve

God my God, above You there is no other. Matchless God You are. Honor and glory is due to You, for Your Majesty is forevermore. Worthy Father, I am not deserving of the depth of love and mercy You have shown to me. You have given me life, health, and countless blessing that money cannot buy, so how can I ever repay You? I am the creation of Your hands, a moulded dust bearing Your Spirit; serving You is the least I can do to express my gratitude for my very existence.

Galatians 5:13 says,
 "For you, brethren, have been called to liberty; only do not use liberty as an

LET US PRAY

opportunity for the flesh, but through love serve one another."

I thank You for the liberty You have given me, and I am committed to availing this opportunity maximally through service. Lord, please give me grace to serve relentlessly. In the scriptures, David charged Solomon saying,

> "As for you, my son Solomon, know the God of your father, and serve Him with a loyal heart and with a willing mind"
> [I Chronicles 28:9].

Lord, to this I subscribe, pledging to serve You willingly and in absolute loyalty. You are a God that searches all hearts and You understand all intent of every thought; see my heart Lord, and know how selfless I have come to commit to serving You.

Matthew 20:26, 28 says,
> "Whoever desires to become great among you, let him be your servant. Just as the Son of Man did not come to be

served, but to serve, and to give His life a ransom for many."

The bible says,
> "So David went to Saul and began serving him. Saul loved David very much, and David became his armor bearer." [1 Samuel 16:21].

Father, I make my choice to serve my way up, look now upon me as Your servant and give me grace for service.

It is is written,
> "If your grace-gift is serving, then thrive in serving others well." [Romans 12:7].

I ask of You dear Lord, the grace-gift to serve as is pleasing unto You my Master. For scripture says,

> "No one serving as a soldier gets entangled in civilian affairs, but rather tries to please his commanding officer." [2 Timothy 2:4].

LET US PRAY

It is also written,

> "Not lagging in diligence, fervent in spirit, serving the Lord." [Romans 12:11].

Help me Lord, to serve diligently, not lagging in anyway, giving no excuse as and when demand is thrust at me to fulfill my service commitment vow; I pray for fervency in the spirit that flesh may not prevail; for flesh cannot fulfill the demands of the spirit.

I desire Lord to serve in humility even as it is written,

> "I served the Lord with great humility." [Acts 20:19a],

so help me my Father. I want to serve You selflessly without an ulterior motive for gain, for the scripture says,

> "Not by compulsion but willingly, not for dishonest gain but eagerly." [I Peter 5:2b].

LET US PRAY

Father, disallow the spirit of Gehazi in me, O Lord my God. I pray my motive of service remains pure, that I might not end like Judas who sold his place in Your kingdom for 30 pieces of silver as the bible says,

> "The devil having already put it into the heart of Judas Iscariot, Simon's son, to betray Him," [John 13:2].

Jehovah, I want to serve You all of my days with joy and gladness that my portion may not be as it is written in Deuteronomy 28:47,

> "Because you did not serve the LORD your God with joy and gladness of heart, for the abundance of everything."

Lord I ask, please lace me with the joy of serving, and the gladness to serve. The Bible says,

> "Those who have served well as deacons obtain for themselves a good standing and great boldness in the faith which is in Christ Jesus." [I Timothy 3:13].

LET US PRAY

It is my prayer that I will serve you so well by Your bestowed grace that I may obtain for myself a good standing with Jesus Christ and that my faith in Him may become daringly bold.

In Exodus 23:25, the scripture says,
> "So you shall serve the LORD your God, and He will bless your bread and your water. And I will take sickness away from the midst of you."

Deuteronomy 11:13-14 says,
> "So if you faithfully obey the commands...... to love the Lord your God and to serve him with all your heart and with all your soul— then I will send rain on your land in its season, both autumn and spring rains, so that you may gather in your grain, new wine and olive oil."

Covenant keeping God, I humbly ask, match Your word in my life as I dutifully serve You; give me health and wealth that I might yet be strong and able to serve you all of my days. Rain down Your blessing upon me and cause me to lack nothing

LET US PRAY

that my life may glorify You, even as other people see that serving You is worth every inch of it. All of these I ask in the name of Your precious son Jesus Christ.

And now Father, consecrate me, as I present my heart of service and pledge my allegiance to serve; for You did same to Aaron in Exodus 29:44,

> "So I...will consecrate Aaron and his sons to serve me as priests."

I thank You for counting me in as Your servant.

NOTES

TESTIMONY

Grace For Humility

Almighty and Everlasting God, to You be honor and glory and praise. The blessedness of Your name is incomprehensible. I salute Your Majesty. Great are You God and You deserve to be greatly praised; from my core I praise You mighty Father. You are God all by Yourself, and incomparable to none; as it is written,

> "None can compare to you among the gods, O Lord! Your exploits are incomparable! For you are great and do amazing things. You alone are God." [Psalms 86:8,10].

LET US PRAY

Be glorified heavenly Lord in the name of Jesus Christ. High and Highly exalted One, the Bible says in Isaiah 57:15,

> "For thus says the High and Lofty One Who inhabits eternity, whose name is Holy: "I dwell in the high and holy place, With him who has a contrite and humble spirit, To revive the spirit of the humble, And to revive the heart of the contrite ones.""

You dwell on high yet you dwell with the lowly in heart. Your word says "He gives more grace. Therefore He says:

> "God resists the proud, But gives grace to the humble." [James 4:6 NKJV].

Pride is repulsive to You my Lord, hence you oppose the proud. The Bible even says,

> "Pride goes before destruction, And a haughty spirit before a fall."
> [Proverbs 16:18].

LET US PRAY

Lord, I come with total resolve and submission as one whose delight is to do Your Will, for,

> "My nourishment comes from doing the will of God..." [John 4:34].

I choose to walk the path of humility, for:

> "Pride leads to disgrace, but with humility comes wisdom." [Proverbs 11:2].

I want wisdom, I therefore humble myself before You; for the scripture says,

> "So humble yourselves under the mighty power of God, and at the right time he will lift you up in honor." [1 Peter 5:6].

Psalms 149:4 says,
> "For the Lord delights in his people; he crowns the humble with victory."

Psalms 25:9 also says
> "He leads the humble in doing right, teaching them his way."

LET US PRAY

Psalms 101:5b states that,
   "I will not endure conceit and pride."

Jehovah I choose the path of humility, I have come to be rid of every deposit and dominance of pride in me. Any iota of pride in me I ask that it be flushed out of me now in the name of Jesus Christ.

Isaiah 2:11 says,
   "Human pride will be brought down, and human arrogance will be humbled. Only the Lord will be exalted on that day of judgment."

   "For all those who exalt themselves will be humbled, and those who humble themselves will be exalted." [Luke 14:11].

Father, it is required of me in wisdom to humble myself and exactly that Lord, is what I have chosen to do. I choose to be modest, I embrace a courteous living, I clasp unto meekness even like Moses, for Numbers 12:3 says,

LET US PRAY

"(Now Moses was very humble—more humble than any other person on earth.)"

I choose to emulate Apostle Paul by,
"Serving the Lord with all humility as stated in Acts 20:19.

I follow Jesus, I choose to walk in the steps of Him who said,

"Take my yoke upon you and learn from me, for I am gentle and humble in heart, and you will find rest for your souls." [Matthew 11:29].

I choose to be like Jesus; I follow His lead, for

"Though he was God, he did not think of equality with God as something to cling to. Instead, he gave up his divine privileges; he took the humble position of a slave and was born as a human being. When he appeared in human form, he humbled himself in obedience

LET US PRAY

to God and died a criminal's death on a cross." [Philippians 2:6-8].

Henceforth in my life, I take on the humble position, Father God help me, keep me, sustain my resolve and cause me to receive the reward of humility for,

> "The reward for humility and fear of the Lord is riches and honor and life." [Proverbs 22:4].

Thank You dear Lord for answering my intentional and humble prayer in the name of Jesus Christ. Amen.

NOTES

TESTIMONY

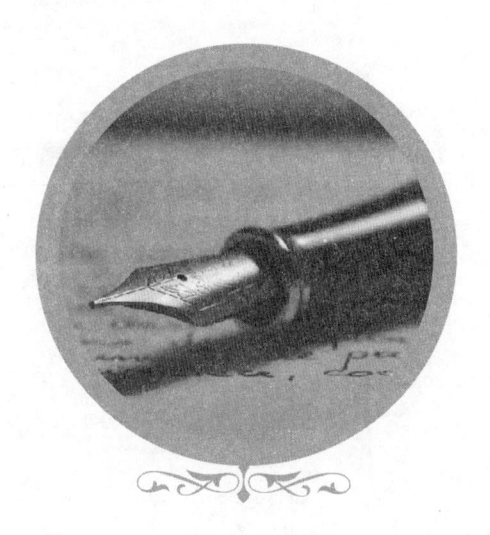

In Closing

Beloved of God, it is my belief that as you have spoken into the ears of God [reading through this book], so will the Lord Almighty, the prayer answering God do to You in the name of Jesus Christ.

In the introduction section of this book, I called attention to the fact that, prayer is expected to be an ongoing practice, a continuous lifestyle. Jesus one day made his disciples realize that prayer is not a one off or rarely done practice. He said Prayer must be ongoing Luke 18:1 (NKJV)

> "Then He spoke a parable to them, that men always ought to pray and not lose heart,".

LET US PRAY

Prayer is not designed by God to be something you engage only when there is a "fire on the mountain" situation in your life; neither is it merely a "give me, give me" channel. Prayer is communicating with God. I therefore encourage you to keep the fire on your prayer altar burning.

This book as mentioned at the onset, is designed to encourage you to pray with result and thereby alleviate the frustration that many encounter in prayer.

Having prayed expediently, as you read through this book, I encourage you to keep at it, knowing fully well this book is limited on the manner and dimensions of prayer that should be prayed through your life time. This book [and the series of same that will yet be released as the Lord gives grace], shall serve only to wet your appetite; with an intent to get you stirred up, inspired and tuned on to hit the throne of grace creatively without the usual pressure and burden many feel when it comes to prayer.

LET US PRAY

I beseech you to continue to

> "...Pray passionately in the Spirit, as you constantly intercede with every form of prayer at all times. [Ephesians 6:18 TPT].

> Keep on "rejoicing in hope, patient in tribulation, continuing steadfastly in prayer..." [Romans 12:12].

Be reminded that the scripture says in Matthew 21:22 (NKJV)

> "And whatever things you ask in prayer, believing, you will receive."

For it is written in I John 5:14-15 (NKJV)

> "...this is the confidence that we have in Him, that if we ask anything according to His will, He hears us. And if we know that He hears us, whatever we ask, we know that we have the petitions that we have asked of Him."

LET US PRAY

May the Lord answer all your prayers." [Psalms 20:5b NLT].

"I entrust you into God's hands and the message of his grace, which is all that you need to become strong. All of God's blessings are imparted through the message of his grace, which he provides as the spiritual inheritance given to all of his holy ones." [Acts 20:32 TPT]

Remain Victorious!

Deepen Your Walk With God With

TO ORDER YOUR COPY OF DEFINING MOMENT DEVOTIONAL

CALL: +234 802 990 8923

Mayokun Oreofe Ministry Official Line

NOTES

TESTIMONY

NOTES

TESTIMONY